the volunteer's
BACK POCKET
GUIDE TO
events & retreats

NECESSITIES FOR VOLUNTEER LEADERS

BY JOHNNY SCOTT

The Volunteer's Back Pocket Guide to Youth Events and Retreats
Necessities for Volunteer Leaders

Copyright © 2011 Christ in Youth

group.com
simplyyouthministry.com

Credits
Author: Johnny Scott
Executive Developer: Nadim Najm
Chief Creative Officer: Joani Schultz
Copy Editor: Rob Cunningham
Cover Art and Production: Riley Hall and Veronica Lucas
Production Manager: DeAnne Lear

Unless otherwise indicated, all Scripture quotations are taken from the Holy Bible, New Living Translation, copyright © 1996, 2004, 2007. Used by permission of Tyndale House Publishers, Inc., Carol Stream, Illinois 60188. All rights reserved.

ISBN 978-0-7644-6528-4

10 9 8 7 6 5 4 3 2 1   20 19 18 17 16 15 14 13 12 11

Printed in the United States of America.

CONTENTS

Introduction 1

1. Preparing for Your Event or Retreat 1

2. Some Thoughts for When You're in the Thick of It 5

3. Rules and Regulations 15

4. Thoughts for New Volunteers 19

5. Thoughts for Veteran Volunteers 27

6. Leader to Leader 31

7. What Do You Do When the Unexpected Happens 35

8. For Volunteers' Eyes Only 39

9. Don't Be This Person 41

10. Special Situations That Will Come Up 47

11. The Landing 51

12. Wrapping It Up 57

INTRODUCTION

(Supplies? Check. Energy drinks? Check. Teenagers? Check. WAIT! Read this book first!)

Events, camps, retreats, and similar experiences seem so intertwined to youth ministry culture that we can't imagine working with teenagers and not announcing some upcoming activity. It's what we do constantly: Teach the lesson and then make the announcements! "Don't forget, we are visiting the old folks' home Saturday—and turn in your registration for camp!" These tools have become catalytic platforms to starting relationships with teenagers and inviting them into relationship with Jesus. However, it's not the events on a youth ministry calendar that will shape and define the culture of a group as much as it is the leaders that go on them with the students!

This book is a dynamic collection of thoughts about different kinds of events you may find yourself on: the weekend retreat, the video game marathon, the amusement park road trip, the summer camp, or the specially themed outreach your group eagerly anticipates. You'll find specific tools and information that will aid you in each of these situations. Some of the material may be pointed toward one kind of event while other general principles can be applied to many of the activities common to youth ministries.

If you are reading this book because you have an upcoming event where you have the chance to work with teenagers, then I am so excited for you. What a privilege. In fact, it's also part of God's desire for us as Christians, parents, or anyone else entrusted to spend time with teenagers. Here's what Psalm 78:4 says: *We will not hide these truths from our children; we will tell the next generation about the glorious deeds of the Lord, about his power and his mighty wonders.*

Anytime you're with teenagers, it's a chance to make a significant investment in their lives. You are building bridges for conversations that are to come. Just as significantly, you are modeling a faith that will lead to breakthroughs in their lives you may never even know about. It is my hope that your time reflecting over these thoughts on interacting with teenagers during retreats and events will equip you to better maximize your impact.

Important! Before you hang with students for any event or even before you read the rest of this book, will you agree to prayerfully consider the mysterious experience of teenagers developing their faith in conjunction with caring adults outside their normal routine? You need to believe in the powerful way God works outside the lines. Think back to the events and special occasions you participated in when you were younger. Did you count down the days to a spring break celebration? Did retreats or camps with leaders and friends from your church play a role in your decision to follow Christ—or to take your faith journey seriously? Is that why you are willing to pitch in and give back now? Or perhaps your story was quite different: You didn't have the opportunity to participate in such events when you were a teenager, but you recognize their impact and value. Whatever the case, may your time reading this book prepare you not just to survive but also to thrive!

Why do we do events and retreats anyway?

The short answer: because they are fun and teenagers remember them. However, there are some deeper reasons that every leader should remember so in the heat of the moment you can remind yourself why you have aged four years in 72 hours.

Everybody needs a break from the mundane or something to look forward to—including teenagers! We live in an age of hurried children that are shuttled from one activity to the next, and students can benefit from interruptions to their routines. Besides the family, only the church is equipped to provide an environment where teenagers can search out their faith with caring adults. The church is the place where we invite students to holistically experience all the great things in life together that God intended. Sure, it can be awkward at times because teenagers don't know all the social cues or rules yet—like the value of wearing deodorant! But these moments with students very well may be the mountaintops of their teenage years. These shared experiences can be big steps in a world of baby steps.

Not everyone believes in the power of events or retreats. Every now and then a magazine article or opinion will come along claiming that they're a thing of the past. While it's true that youth culture is continually changing and our moments with students seem to be dwindling, the benefits of breaking the norm are huge. Simply put, teenagers seem to be more open in many areas of their lives when their routines are interrupted.

Since the emergence of modern youth ministry, retreats and events have been a standard part of the curriculum because they're part of the coming-of-age experience. The greatest stories of all time are filled with distant lands, dangerous passages (we try to avoid those as much as possible), hidden fortune, and great escapes. We are drawn to these powerful stories because they resonate with a need and longing deep inside of us. I would even argue that it reflects part of who God is, which is why it echoes within us. We can all hope that our spiritual journeys will ultimately look more like a great adventure than a series of systematically calculated steps!

Events and retreats are so important because they allow us to advance. When we make a time and place to "retreat," we are taking refuge from the regular onslaught of our hectic lives to examine our perspective. With new perspective, we can move forward with renewed energy and purpose. Here are two ways that these new perspectives launch us forward—and God uniquely designs both results.

First, people change on an individual level when they "retreat." We all need sparks that propel us in our own personal journey with Jesus, and special events are often the framework for that to happen. It may not manifest itself clearly in the moment. Perhaps days or weeks later, after teenagers have returned to their routines, they are overwhelmed with a sudden realization— but the seed for that pivotal life change was fostered in the framework of an event or retreat.

Our communal story is the second perspective that God can shape during an event or trip. Just like we each have our own set of circumstances that define who and where we are on our spiritual journey, our community travels the path of a spiritual journey, too. As individuals we may be getting along fine, but the health of the whole group is off. Our community can experience blessing through an event or retreat. God uses the time, space, and intentionality of a well-planned event or retreat to be the spark that moves members of a community closer together and closer to himself.

God understands the need for a good trek; in fact many times, God initiated *spiritual* movement through *physical* trips. God called Abraham to pick up and go to a distant land—a destination unknown! God called Moses back to Egypt, leading a *huge* group to a camp he was going to build for them (I'm paraphrasing only slightly for the point). Jesus called 12 men on a three-year road trip that would change the course of human history forever. Our eternal calling is a lifelong trip where we are reconciled to God. I'm pretty sure there will still be moments like ice cream outings. And those won't be "for fun only" then either.

Whether it is a special occasion at the church or an adventurous weekend gathering at the beach or in the mountains, these moments have the potential to set foundations of faith. You will get to be there when special memories are made that affect lives and generations to come. There is no such thing as a "for fun only" trip when spiritually intentional adults are along for the ride. Let's get busy equipping you to be a passionate volunteer ready to thrive. This is going to be a great adventure!

CHAPTER

I

PREPARING FOR YOUR EVENT OR RETREAT

Leading teenagers is not an easy task, and like any important job, it takes a sense of preparation on many levels. How you prepare for an experience can greatly determine its outcome. Jesus provides a great example of preparing for ministry. Before he started his ministry, he took off into the wilderness by himself to be alone with God the Father. It was apparent that the road ahead was going to be difficult and that the careful preparation was essential for him and his mission. Satan knew that this period of reflection and readiness would be a perfect time to attack Jesus, so he did. Your investment in teenagers can make a significant impact. Satan knows this and may attack you as you prepare. Read Matthew 4:1-11 to see what Jesus did to prepare himself for ministry. Here are some other thoughts on preparing before your event or retreat!

Take time to pray

If you spend time praying *before* your event or retreat, you will have time to cover all the prayers that seem logical, ordinary, and appropriate. This is important because at youth events, you may find yourself praying for and about things that you never thought any person would ever pray for in the course of the human experience. Don't understand what I mean? At a weekend retreat, you may find yourself praying, "God, help that boy not kill the cat in the pillowcase when he hits the other teenager that I'm not sure is even part of our group." Prayers like this may cause guilt if they are the first prayers you have uttered in some time. So pray before your event for things like spiritual impact for the students attending, strength for the other leaders, wisdom and discernment from the Holy Spirit (see James 4), and God's work in the families represented by the teenagers.

Be physically ready

Don't fool yourself: Getting ready physically shouldn't only concern out-of-shape or older youth workers. Trips and retreats (and even one-day events) can be demanding. Don't underestimate the toll this can take on your body! If you are over 19 years old, out of high school, and have played a video game for over four hours in one sitting, I am talking to *you*! The human body is not meant to go with less than three hours of sleep on the floor, surviving on Ding Dongs® and Ho Hos® exclusively for sustenance. I've seen college students at the height of their physical specimen go unconscious because they didn't appropriately prepare for a winter retreat. High school students may laugh while you stretch out before playing Capture the Flag. Live with that instead of a nickname like "The Guy Who Died at Summer Camp." Don't start the event tired; rest up before you arrive, and eat healthy before you get there—chances are good that you'll consume Taco Bell® delicacies at least three times, even if the event doesn't last an entire day.

Pack accordingly

If you show up with a fanny pack loaded with sunscreen, you will be made fun of—and then everyone will come to you asking for sunscreen. If you show up to the roller skating party with your own in-line skates, you will be made fun of—and then you will be asked for pointers all night. These are double-edged swords—personal decisions that you, wise adult volunteer, must make on your own. The moral of the story: Within reason, pack the stuff you will need for the specific event, and don't be a kid and forget things—you're an adult, for goodness sake. And no, we don't have time to stop and find a bathroom; we just left the church!

Choose to journey spiritually with the students

This really is a conscious decision. It's similar to telling teenagers to make important decisions *before* they get into a crisis and have to think on their feet. If they have already decided to not do drugs, they have a prepared answer and thought-out commitment in their heart. The same logic applies to us as volunteers. Events and retreats can move fast. Prayerfully make the sober-minded decision to intentionally journey spiritually with your students. That commitment needs to be made beforehand so you can move with the group and, more importantly, the Holy Spirit. The effects of this single decision may be the most important ones you experience. This choice will show up in the nuances of every other fork in the road. And by deciding to be all in, you won't miss out on what God wants to teach *you* along the way, which may end up being as significant as what you intended to teach the teenagers.

Offer support to parents

Like a good sermon, your event or retreat needs a clearly thought-out purpose—and it's essential for communicating that purpose and all the other details to parents. You also want to connect with parents when they bring their teenagers to the church or other location for your event. As a leader, you can do little things to help make this pivotal moment the best it can be! Help calm anxieties—especially if you're leaving for a longer camp or retreat, or if parents are dropping off a first-timer—by serving homemade cookies while kids unload luggage. Make sure you clearly communicate details about traffic, sign-ups, and other items that could stir up nerves that are already tense. Welcoming parents and praying as a group are always good ideas, too. You know your context; create the most appropriate atmosphere possible. The most common mistakes come through poor communication and planning.

CHAPTER 2

SOME THOUGHTS FOR WHEN YOU'RE IN THE THICK OF IT

The journey matters

If your event or trip involves any kind of drive—especially a long trek—then plan some activities, discussions, music, and other "focusing" elements that point to the purpose for your event. For better or for worse, the momentum from the church parking lot to the destination can shape the whole group's attitude. Think ahead on this one and free up enough leaders who are not driving to spearhead the idea so that the drive time is a major part of the event and can be used effectively, too. While teenagers do need downtime and free time to socialize, remain on the lookout for moments when your bag of preplanned "tricks" can keep the community moving in the right direction.

Prepare for immaturity

Cutting-edge brain research reveals that the prefrontal lobe is the last part of the human brain to develop, not fully maturing for most people until they're around 25 years old. (Yes, you most likely have an undeveloped brain if you are younger than 25, and that's part of the reason car rental companies are reluctant to trust you!) The prefrontal lobe is the part of the brain

5

that helps people choose wisely—or more technically, make choices based on previous life experiences while weighing the myriad of possible outcomes. This means someone is going to do something unmentionable. The problem here is that you will have to most likely mention it to their parents and the pastor when you get back home! In these situations, remember that teenagers will be teenagers. While you need to enforce any rules that are established for your event or retreat, choose to see "immature moments" as learning experiences—chances for your teenagers to grow. They will "read you" in search of clues, so be aware of your reactions and body language. Try not to make a bigger deal than necessary out of the situation, and keep your end goal in mind. Many times, your end goal can still be accomplished even when immaturity rears its ugly head.

No matter what, don't knock the parents ever, ever, ever
This can be hard because at times you will see parents do some bonehead things. However wrong a parent may be, they will still be the most significant influence in their child's life. Even in the most difficult of situations our language should never be against the parent. There is a time to intervene between a parent and a child. This should happen when the safety of the child is in question. Always consult the proper authority for laws. Proverbs 18:17 says, *The first to speak in court sounds right—until the cross-examination begins*.

Debrief with your students
Most teenagers won't naturally do this. It is not in their nature to pause and critically think through their experiences. Remember, one of the reasons we offer retreats and events for our students is to create settings that add a spark to our conversations with them. What better way to talk about the way Jesus trained the disciples than around a campfire! "Jesus ate just like this with Peter and John many times!" Here are a few quick pointers about debrief times on trips:

- Frequent and regular debriefing throughout the day may be better than long sessions at the end of the day when everybody is tired.

- Don't get discouraged if debriefing doesn't work at first; you are getting your students acquainted with the concept more than really diving into the content. Give them time to get comfortable, pausing in the midst of the adventure to discuss their thoughts.

- Be OK with asking more questions than you answer at first. It is OK to say, "Let's keep thinking about that as we continue."

- Use this time to encourage your teenagers and show them how they need each other. Always be on the lookout for ways to bring students into this discussion time, and turn to them for conversation launching points when you decide to initiate a debriefing moment.

- Let your students know that you want everyone to participate; don't let the same teenagers dominate the talking, and find ways to engage the students who might try to hide in the crowd.

But also debrief with your leaders
Always leave room for a timeout and for conversations with other leaders at your retreat or event. Gather together and discuss what is going on. Share great things you sense happening, and chat about any concerns you may have. When you go it alone, the outcome is never as good. Other leaders in your group will need your encouragement as much as you need theirs. One word of advice: When you and the other leaders debrief, don't have students nearby—it's important for leaders to experience a safe environment so they can openly discuss things that may

not be appropriate for the teenagers to hear. Take time to pray and ask God to open your eyes to what he is doing on the trip. You will be amazed by the transformation you and other leaders experience through regular debriefings.

I tell leaders before big trips that we have a tradition every night of gathering together as leaders to discuss the day, talk about students who need special attention or students who are not connecting, prepare for the next day, and so on. Sometimes this is a five-minute conversation; sometimes it's 25 minutes. I also use this time to state the obvious and help people relax. If something failed during the day, I bring it up and ask for advice on how we could have done it better. It's a good time to keep everyone updated on student issues and our event schedule, and I always try to make this a time when we can laugh together, tell stories of the day, and just hang with each other.

—A Youth Worker

The power of appropriate touch

It's unfortunate that the subject of physical contact with students is so clouded because of the inappropriate ways some people have used such a potentially beneficial and good thing. We should always use *appropriate* touch in careful ways to protect the students we minister to—whether at an event, retreat, or just an ordinary youth service. When used in a proper and healthy way, human touch can be powerful. A pat on the shoulder or a hug can be a turning point for a teenager who needs the affirmation.

Use side hugs; never do front hugs with members of the opposite sex—and use them judiciously with members of your own gender. Use discretion in knowing when a healthy no-touch rule is best for your context. As a general rule, never touch the opposite sex beyond a side hug. Only use touch in open, public

8

areas where a student (or an observer) would be less likely to misread the gesture. Take into account a teenager's personal story and how he or she might respond to touch. If you are not aware of that student's story, then lean toward a no-touch policy.

Realize that even asking everyone to hold hands and circle up to pray can be an intimate and uncomfortable experience for teenagers—and for adults, too! Such an action could involve deep feelings of commitment to the group and affiliation or even embarrassment. This doesn't mean we shouldn't offer these kinds of experiences; we just need to be aware of what our students may be thinking while we lead or participate in them.

Here are some examples of appropriate and generally safe forms of touch. When talking to guys who are rowdy (could also apply when talking to *any* guy) a hand on the shoulder will generally calm them and help them give undivided attention. The high five (or one of the 147,321 variations of the handshake) is usually a safe option. The "double high five" is usually reserved for celebrations surrounding intense community games. Don't pull this one out to early in a relationship; save it for dodgeball semifinals, at least!

Skip the complaining
If you are going to be an effective youth worker, then actively choose to fight your personal desire to complain. Sure, you'll find lots of things to complain about at an event or retreat, and many of us easily lean in this direction. However, teenagers will take what may be your simple passing comment and carry it to a whole new level. Complaining will lead to dissension and alienation. Complaining can be a poison that continues to grow unless you, other leaders, and the students decide to defeat it. If you know you have a problem with this, then ask other leaders to hold you accountable. Pray often, specifically asking God to

help you defeat a complaining spirit so that everyone at your retreat or event can be free to follow where the Holy Spirit is leading. *Most important of all, continue to show deep love for each other, for love covers a multitude of sins. Cheerfully share your home with those who need a meal or a place to stay. God has given gifts to each of you from his great variety of spiritual gifts. Manage them well so that God's generosity can flow through you (1 Peter 4:8-10).*

Respect your students

That may seem like such simple a statement, but starting without this premise in your heart can destroy a retreat or event. Here's the main idea: Treat your teenagers the way you want to be treated. No, they aren't adults who've been trusted to help lead the trip. However, we must remember that our students are people and interact with them accordingly. Remember what it was like to be a kid in school when there was such a clear line drawn between who was in charge and who wasn't? Teenagers feel like cattle sometimes. They are herded from one place to the next with adults telling them, "Because I said so." Students don't like being herded around, and they can grow to quickly resent people who talk to them disrespectfully. Keeping students informed is important, too. Let them know what's happening next. Communicate well and often—it's an incredible sign of respect. So in the thick of an event or retreat, when things are getting crazy, remind yourself of this simple idea.

Support your leaders

Church leaders aren't perfect; they can make bad decisions. Perhaps your trip leader didn't plan well, and you're carrying the brunt of responsibilities. But the middle of an event or retreat probably isn't the right time to address all of your concerns, even if they're valid. You also may encounter moments when students pick up on issues and talk among themselves negatively.

Never join, start, or encourage this behavior. In the end, it will lead to no good thing. As leaders, we are calling teenagers to know God, love God, and lead a life that honors God. The greatest teaching moment of your event or retreat may be when you model a submissive attitude toward those God has put in authority over you—even if you disagree with a decision or style of leadership. There are, of course, lines that should not be crossed when it comes to the safety of teenagers or other crazy, out-of-bounds activities—and your debriefing times with other leaders are the best opportunities to raise those concerns. But negative talk about leadership will create collateral damage that may not be worth the "win."

Enjoy a break from your plans

Did you know that taking teenagers to Wal-Mart® could be a healthy idea on some trips? Being in a new environment can be difficult for some students to handle. After so many new experiences, they may hit a wall where fatigue sets in. Finding a simple activity—such as going to a store that looks exactly like the one back home—can re-energize them and give them the ability to dive back into the adventure. Obviously, it doesn't have to be a Wal-Mart®, but look for an oasis place or a quick activity that can settle any nerves. Another priority is making sure your students have enough quiet, reflective time figured into every day. Not every student will need the same amount, but a little dose can reset a teenager's ability to have a positive experience.

Talk often about the "why"

The purpose of your event—even if it is a fun outreach with inflatables—needs to be woven into the fabric of all the little mundane elements. Teenagers learn in different ways. Saying the purpose of an activity once may only register with 25 percent of your students, so say things more than once. More

II

ortantly, reiterate the purpose in unique, creative ways. Deuteronomy 11:19-21 says this: *"Teach [these instructions] to your children. Talk about them when you are at home and when you are on the road, when you are going to bed and when you are getting up. Write them on the doorposts of your house and on your gates, so that as long as the sky remains above the earth, you and your children may flourish in the land the Lord swore to give your ancestors."*

Be a participant, not an observer

If you're helping with a '70s dress-up party, then dress up! Be there *completely:* Get the bell-bottoms, the big hair, and the platform shoes, and fully share in the experience. Volunteers who stand on the sidelines end up watching the clock and eventually tap out. It can be hard to tell which action or conversation may lead to a relational breakthrough with a teenager. When we participate, we are telling teenagers contextually that we are "in it" with them. We trust them so much that we will get goofy around them. Eventually, this will be reciprocated by new depth in the friendship.

Make spiritual markers

The simplest things usually work best! Don't miss the profound power of claiming the moments spiritually. When you take a hike, make the summit a spiritual marker by singing a song, or reading a passage from Scripture. Look for opportunities to cement the whole experience of your event or retreat through a faith-building moment. Here are some thoughts on making spiritual markers.

- Whenever possible, make spiritual markers physical— including something each student can take home after the retreat or event.

- Give everyone a chance to participate.

- Model your spiritual markers on a verse or passage of Scripture. Explain the context in the Bible, and relate it to your current situation.

- Make your spiritual marker ceremony memorable, even if the event is small or spontaneous. Do this by getting involvement from your students and other leaders.

- If you can, plan ahead and let your teenagers know that something special will take place. Give them the chance to prepare something for the occasion.

- Give students an opportunity for solitude after your spiritual marker ceremony.

Focus on the new experiences

As a volunteer, you have the ability to help set the tone for your retreat or event. Be aware of new students and their assimilation into the group. Be cautious about inside jokes and references to the "good ol' days." Many teenagers will gravitate toward these discussions, and they are appropriate at times. They're reminders of lessons that are learned communally and remembered communally. Frame these conversations in such a way that invites newcomers into the experience. Keep the goal of your trip at the forefront so no one misses out on the new lessons God wants to reveal. Both new and veteran students need these fresh experiences. Help them by guiding the group's attention to the experience that is at hand.

Go for the "Molesky"

Every volunteer needs to know the time to pull out a well-polished "we are not done with this retreat yet" pep talk—or a "Molesky." A properly timed Molesky can pivot the direction or refocus an entire group. An effective Molesky might be words of encouragement, perspective on what we have experienced thus far, correction if needed, and inspiration to finish strong. Resist the urge to overuse this powerful tool. Also use discretion in determining if the Molesky is best for an individual or the entire group.

Choose to invest in a life
Be praying for one teenager specifically; you can't pastor or influence all of them, and that is fine, but choose to invest in the life of one teenager at your retreat or event. It's not up to you to make a difference in every student's life. Don't be consumed with your schedule or agenda. Many teenagers want to see their lives changed as much as you want God to use you in the process. There is a natural process to learning and growing. This often works best when you walk with teenagers through the journey. Sit back, trust God, and love students.

CHAPTER
3

RULES AND REGULATIONS

considering how anarchy can reign if rules are never established or enforced, you might want to read these thoughts!

Let's be honest: Creating and enforcing rules is one of the least enjoyable parts of youth ministry—but establishing boundaries is essential for ensuring that your students have a safe, meaningful, enjoyable experience at your retreat or event.

Quick thoughts on rules

- Communicate rules in advance and in writing to students *and* parents—and communicate the consequences of violating the rules, including the possibility of being sent home early.

- Consider the attitude in which you give the rules. Try to keep "negative" rules (the don'ts) to a minimum. Instead, phrase them in a positive way as much as possible.

- Offer rules in a biblical light—not being good just for goodness' sake but because it honors God.

- Treat students with respect as you create and enforce rules.

- Don't create a rule that you don't plan or want to enforce.

- Rules should serve your purpose, so evaluate your rules in light of that goal.

- Consider rules for vehicle travel that help promote safe environments. For example: Driving through the night? Keep lights on, and separate the genders.

- Plan enough options and good activities for your group. This will help greatly by giving teenagers things they can do instead of inventing their own activities—and increasing the likelihood of violating a rule or two.

Here are a few more detailed thoughts on unique rule-related issues you might face during events and retreats. As a volunteer, you may not be the person creating the rules, but it's always valuable to think through the rationale behind guidelines and boundaries.

Rules on smoking
Decide ahead of time what your policy will be for teenagers who are already addicted to nicotine. Will you let them smoke? If so, will you establish any boundaries on when and where they can smoke? Is it more important to keep tobacco rules enforced or to have a student attend who would not be able to otherwise in a reasonable frame of mind? And if you do permit students to smoke, how will you communicate this to the other teenagers— and parents and church leaders?

Rules against bullying
There is no room for bullying on a trip. Bullying is one of the single biggest challenges teenagers face today. Even when students seem to be getting along, some may be caught in stressful situations that require a leader's involvement. Be on

the lookout. Even "good kids" can be mean sometimes. When you sign up to be a volunteer, you are agreeing to be a leader, and parents are counting on you to look after the best interests of their children. Bullying hurts everyone: those who bully, those who get bullied, and those who allow it to continue. Create clear rules against bullying behavior—and enforce them.

Rules on sneaking out

Many of your teenagers will want to sneak out late at night. Some will actually attempt it. This is part of the adventure of a retreat or camp or overnight event, and many times the legend of past great "sneak-out moments" fuels the students' desire. Here's a different perspective on this issue: Let them sneak out—but don't let them do it alone. Plan it, go with them, make it an intentional event, and invite everyone in the circle, not just the three students you like best. Because these moments can be monumental, *don't waste them*. Plan a spiritual marker or destination with meaning. Let other adults know what is going on. Never go "Lone Ranger" on this type of excursion, and always plan ahead on safety. But remember: If your youth pastor or key leaders say absolutely no sneaking out, then submit and follow their lead.

Reasons to send a student home

This can be a difficult but necessary decision, and it typically involves violation of rules established for the event or retreat. If students and parents haven't agreed that certain violations could lead to this consequence, sending a student home might create more problems than it resolves. As a volunteer, it's unlikely that you'll be the person making the final decision on sending a student home, but here are some guidelines to keep in mind when this option is on the table.

- Talk with the student; always bring along at least one other adult as a witness.

17

- Examine the student's intent.

- Follow guidelines and consequences that were established and explained before the event or retreat. Never complain about what you permit.

- Consider the home situation; will sending this student home lead to unwanted consequences?

- How will this impact the entire group?

I always invite parents to our pre-trip meeting because at the beginning I quickly go over a few ground rules, and the first one is what will get you sent home. And by "sent home" I mean your family is responsible to pick you up. It does not matter if you have to drive 100 miles or 5 miles—you will not be riding home with us. If we have to, we will purchase a cab, airfare, or some other means of transportation, and bill the family. But we cover this in our consent form, all parents who are regulars know this about our ministry policy, and we cover it at our pre-trip meeting. Don't send a student home if you have never talked about this to parents; always give them examples of situations that are "send-a-student-home-worthy" so when it happens it is not out of the blue or a shock. You never want a parent to say this was never talked about.
—A Youth Leader

CHAPTER 4

THOUGHTS FOR NEW VOLUNTEERS

but veterans are wise enough to read this for a refresher, right?

If you are new to working with teenagers, then you need to know this truth: You can make a huge impact right away. It's true. But you also unintentionally may make some big mistakes that can be avoided. This section will give you some general thoughts that are good for all volunteers to remember when working with teenagers during events and retreats.

Keep in mind that you have a powerful asset because you have constant access to the Holy Spirit! That's right, you are equipped with the greatest counselor who ever was or will be. As you read through these thoughts for new volunteers, tap into the wisdom and discernment available through the Holy Spirit.

Observe the veterans

Let's start with a foundational idea: If you want to learn, pay attention to the people who have the answers! Ask experienced volunteers for advice. Pair up with a veteran youth worker to see how he or she interacts with students. There is no shame in this; it's actually a wise way to grow as a leader. Proverbs 13:13-15 says this: *People who despise advice are asking for trouble;*

those who respect a command will succeed. The instruction of the wise is like a life-giving fountain; those who accept it avoid the snares of death. A person with good sense is respected; a treacherous person is headed for destruction.

Reject the myths about younger volunteers

Age isn't an automatic predictor of how well you'll work with teenagers. God doesn't have a minimum age requirement for working in his kingdom! If you're young, you can make a difference. Throughout the Bible, we read about times God called young people to do important tasks: Isaiah, Jeremiah, David, Mary, and Samuel were all in their youth when God used them. But don't fall into the trap of thinking your youth is an automatic ace card for some Youth Worker of the Year award. Don't assume you will connect with teenagers just because you're close to their age. Your long-term effectiveness as a leader isn't connected to your "cool" status; it's about your heart. Be respectful and encouraging to the veteran volunteers you serve with. It is true that the more you learn and grow as a youth worker, the more effective you will be, but it all starts with having the right attitude and being willing to serve! Learn from the veterans, and do your best to downplay any self-deprecating talk they may verbalize about their ability to work with teenagers due to their age. We all need each other. Welcome to the team!

Don't try to be a friend only

Teenagers already have friends, but most lack mentors and healthy role models. This is a common pitfall that new volunteers make. You can be friendly, but there are differences between you and the students, and those differences exist for a good reason. Don't blur the lines. Sometimes we have to make tough calls as leaders, and our ultimate motivation must be to help guide a teenager toward a Jesus-centered life.

I always use this phrase with my youth leaders: "You have to care more about the friend than the friendship." Sometimes the choices we make are the best thing for the friend to hear, but we know it may hurt our friendship for a season. It's worth the lost season of friendship to make a lasting impact on a student's life. Plus, many teenagers will forget about it in a week and be back to normal.

"Props" can open the door to honest conversation
I have a friend who always carries plenty of extra nail polish with her on trips, camps, and retreats—not because she's vain but because it's a great way for her to make a connection with girls. She makes it known without being pushy that she would love to paint nails and get to know the girls during the trip (yes, this would be a girl-*only* "prop"). Think of something that fits your personality and makes it easier for you to approach teenagers— without being like the awkward van guy asking, "Hey kid, want some candy?" I've seen leaders use card tricks, sports, guitars, and video games. As long as it is not a stretch for you to pull off, it will usually be accepted and work as a bridge to getting to know students. One word of warning: Be authentic. Don't become someone or something you are not. Similarly, don't dress and talk like a teenager in an effort to gain acceptance. This usually backfires and takes way more effort than it's worth!

How do you respond to that question?
Be honest when you don't know the answer to any questions a student asks. You don't have to be a Bible scholar to have a meaningful impact on teenagers. Here is a secret from the veterans: *Many times they don't have the answers to students' questions either!* That fact should lift the undue pressure you face about having all the answers. If you can't answer a question, say something like this: "I don't know, so let's find out the answer together." Teaching teenagers that you don't have to

be a rocket scientist to follow Jesus is a huge gift. This approach works out well in the long run because you have the opportunity to teach students how to find answers to their questions. Model good ways to get answers through God's Word and from other spiritual leaders.

How do you begin a conversation?
A great tip for breaking the ice with teenagers at an event is to simply smile. By smiling you will be communicating many positive nonverbal cues. Smiles are disarming and set a welcomed tone for engaging students in a way that helps them feel safe. Good questions are also highly effective.

Sometimes if I don't know the student that well or don't know what to say in a certain situation, I will ask, "Who are your roommates this weekend?" or "What are you missing at home this weekend?" or "What are you not missing from home this weekend?" or "Have you been to this before?"

Learn students' names
This may seem like a simple tip for connecting with teenagers at an event, but you can build a solid foundation for all your interactions by addressing them as the wonderful individuals they are. There is no sweeter sound to a teenager seeking acceptance, affinity, and identity than the sound of his or her own name.

Don't make fun of their music (or clothes or hair or...)
Their music is probably different from yours. Their clothes are probably different from yours. Their hairstyles may be different from yours. That's OK—they're teenagers, and you're an adult. Resist the temptation to mock their choices, even if they seem ridiculous to you. The "cool" points you think you are earning with other adults are not worth it. Your jokes will rarely turn

teenagers into a fan of your music—yes, even Def Leppard (sad but true). Watch what you model. *Keep a close watch on how you live and on your teaching. Stay true to what is right for the sake of your own salvation and the salvation of those who hear you (1 Timothy 4:16).*

Be sensitive to clues
Some or most of the teenagers are struggling with something. Even the students you think have it all together may be struggling. Perhaps it is their parents' divorce, or low self-esteem, or depression, or addictions, or stress, or a host of other issues. Keep your eyes open to the mood swings. Look for nonverbal language; their mood last night might not reveal where they are emotionally this morning. Give room and be respectful.

Recognize when you need a breather
Youth ministry in general is a marathon. You likely won't see immediate results when working with teenagers. However, retreats and events can be little sprints within the marathon. Just be aware that there is no prize for "crashing" on the journey. Know what you can handle. If you need a breather, then tell a fellow volunteer and look for an opportunity to escape for a few minutes—or a little longer. Good team members will want you in this for the long haul. Keep in touch with where your reserves are, and if needed, catch a breather.

Remember to listen
Learn how to recognize when you've earned the right to ask on a sincere "mask-less" level how a student is doing. Ask in an environment where the teenager has the privacy and time to be honest. Give the student time to fully articulate an answer—and then don't problem solve. Just be there, in the moment. If

some issue is so glaring that you must make a timely comment that can't wait, give the student a simple thought and not a full discourse. You have to earn the right to listen again in the future.

Don't waste a meal
People naturally lower many barriers during an informal meal setting. Plus, sharing a meal can be a very spiritual experience. We all need food to survive, so when we share a meal, we are sharing life-giving substance. Ask your students for permission to sit with them. Don't be afraid to guide the conversation with such topics as "tell me more about who you are." Adults may think of meals as opportunities for a break, but choose to view these times as opportunities to build relationships. Try to schedule your personal breaks when students are engaged in other activities. Take full advantage of meal times!

Let water be your best friend
Water is the best precaution to likely physical problems teenagers may experience on trips, retreats, or events that keep them active. Monitor your group, and urge students to drink water whenever possible. Sickness can slow the progress of the entire event, and it can be a deterrent to well-laid plans. And in the midst of leading, make sure *you* drink enough water, too!

Encourage balance
Use caution not to take advantage of teenagers' propensity toward overly emotional moments when on retreats or at special events. You want your students to experience transformation and change, but maintain a delicate balance. I'm not saying emotions should be rejected or ignored. The expression of sincere emotions has its place, but an overemphasis on displaying emotions can quickly become a bigger goal than what was originally intended. Intense subjects or elements may need to be broken up through the course of your retreat or

event. Don't elevate extreme emotional responses as something valued above all other responses because, like yawning, tears can spread like wildfire among teenagers. I'm all for a good group hug from time to time; just don't let emotional peaks become the standard by which you measure the success of a retreat or event.

CHAPTER 5

THOUGHTS FOR VETERAN VOLUNTEERS

but everyone else can peek—just keep quiet about it

If you've survived in the trenches of youth ministry, then you've learned that spending your energy on trying to be cool isn't the way to invest in teenagers—but that doesn't mean you should swing to the other end of the pendulum, either! Take some time to learn something new about youth culture. Go back to being a student! Continue to be yourself, but be willing to show teenagers in some practical way that your age hasn't killed the youthful spirit in your soul.

Remember your first love
It can be easy to fall into the trap of doing things because it's in our routine. Over time these things come to define us, and changing our patterns can require more work than maintaining the status quo. God wants you to serve from the perspective of joy, not one of blind obedience or stagnation. Keep that in mind as you head into your event or retreat. You've had meaningful experiences at these kinds of events before—experiences that have fueled you through the valleys. Those mountaintop moments with teenagers serve as gifts from God on this side of eternity. They remind us of our commitment and what hangs

in the balance. We don't always get to see the seeds we plant. We don't always get to follow through to the harvest. Take some time to remember the precious moments you have had in youth ministry, and ask God to give you some fresh moments at this next event or retreat. The longer you serve, the more tightly you must cherish those moments. Remember the moments when God first affirmed in you the calling to invest in teenagers. Galatians 6:9 offers this word of encouragement: *So let's not get tired of doing what is good. At just the right time we will reap a harvest of blessing if we don't give up.*

Know when to take a break
Healthy volunteers that have shown the ability to stick with this calling protect their hearts by knowing when to refresh themselves. If you have said to yourself that you are only serving because nobody else will, then take some time to examine your heart. Don't serve with a bitter attitude. It may start off in little, subtle comments, but they can become a poison that destroys you and those around you. Maybe you want to skip this next retreat or event and spend some quality time alone with God—or perhaps you simply want to serve in a less demanding role this time around. That would still allow you to support your leaders and serve the students, while personally experiencing some spiritual growth at the retreat or event. Simply commit to always serving with a Christ-like attitude and knowing when you need a break so you can rediscover or maintain that attitude. Deuteronomy 15:10 says this: *"Give generously to the poor, not grudgingly, for the Lord your God will bless you in everything you do."*

Reject the myths about older volunteers
God doesn't have an age cutoff limit for doing his kingdom work. In fact, God called the first great youth leader in our faith, Moses, to take a huge group of children and teenagers on a

40-year trip when he was 80 years old. (Remember: The entire older generation died before the Hebrews finally crossed the Jordan into the Promised Land.) Working for God and with students has everything to do with obedience to your personal calling and nothing to do with age. The more you learn and grow as a youth worker, the more effective you can be! It's tragic to see volunteers who have years of experience and skills bow out of student ministry because they no longer feel in touch. So what if you can't hike up the hill as fast as you used to on hiking trips? Teenagers really don't care. (Most of them enjoy being faster, anyway!) You can be an effective volunteer and do this for the long haul. Perhaps your role will change, and maybe you'll take on different responsibilities at the upcoming event or retreat, but don't walk away—the younger leaders need your guidance, and the teenagers need examples of faith from every walk and stage of life.

Evaluate your traditions
If your upcoming event or retreat is something your youth ministry has done before, take time to evaluate the traditions associated with it. Some traditions can be healthy and add tons of value to your event. But familiarity also can breed contempt. Carefully analyze which elements could continue as healthy traditions that encourage and build up your teenagers, and steer clear of elements that might turn sour. I'm convinced that there is not a group of people more traditional than teenagers. (Old people get a terrible rap on this and deserve our apologies.) Try changing something on students and see the mass coup uprising; it usually only takes about three seconds for them to turn into a mob. However, these same teenagers who want it to be "just like last year" also will quickly say, "We already did this." It's a fine line to walk. Follow the lead of your key leaders as you find a healthy balance between meaningful traditions and fresh experiences—but as a veteran volunteer, also offer your leaders insight and perspective on what to keep and what to drop.

CHAPTER 6

LEADER TO LEADER

we are in this together! i'm going left; you go right. only refer to me by my airsoft name on the field: the exterminator!

Celebrate one another

When students arrive at your event or retreat, it takes all hands on deck. You probably don't have time to communicate effectively with other volunteers when you're in the middle of spit wad wars or really organized small groups talking about deep spiritual concepts. (Obviously, I'm referring to *your* youth group in that second example.) But look for those moments when you and other leaders can gather together, even if for just a couple of minutes, during downtimes to connect with each other and refuel.

It really takes a team of adult volunteers to make a great youth ministry—and a great youth event! Look for the different giftedness in one another, and then celebrate it by using words of affirmation, listening to each other, praying together, and thanking God that you get to do ministry in community. God will bless a loving community with more creativity, peace, and fruit. Rarely do self-seeking ministry cultures attract a steady stream of spiritually healthy volunteers. Leaders who celebrate each other do so because they make time for it. If the community experience of the adult leadership is overflowing with the Fruit of the Spirit, then the students will surely get blessed, too!

Look out for one another's best interests
Because retreats and events are out of the ordinary, be on extra guard for other leaders in these special situations. During your normal youth service contexts, you probably have procedures and clearly defined rules. When it's a special event in a new environment, out-of-the-ordinary can become the ordinary. So tell someone where you are going and what you will do there and when you will be back. Then take more than one person with you for extra help and accountability. Communicate well and frequently about any challenges arising. And if you're a female leader and you see a young lady who appears clingy with a male volunteer or wants private counseling time, take the initiative and step in—you'll help to remove a challenging situation and to protect the integrity of your youth ministry.

Handle conflict well
Retreats and events can get exhausting. Leaders want to know that they have a place on the team and that their contribution is appreciated. Situations can get intense and feelings get hurt when we work with people. We expect to have to navigate this when working with teenagers, and it's no different when we disagree with other leaders. Many issues can be resolved by simply not taking ourselves so seriously. Teenagers will watch how you deal with conflict. How you handle conflict with other leaders may be the most important lesson you get to teach at this event.

Sometimes disagreements run deep and we need a game plan that works. If your conflict is rooted in how something is being handled, then make a decision to publicly defend and privately confront. In Matthew 18:15-17, we see a clear plan from Jesus on how to handle confrontation and conflict: *"If another believer sins against you, go privately and point out the offense. If the other person listens and confesses it, you have won that person back. But if you are unsuccessful, take one or two others with you and go back again, so that everything you say may be confirmed by two or three witnesses. If the person still refuses to listen, take your case to the church. Then if he or she won't accept the church's decision, treat that person as a pagan or a corrupt tax collector."*

Have one another's backs
Don't let students talk maliciously about other leaders behind their backs. Never encourage, agree, or stand by silently when dissension is brewing. *Hatred stirs up quarrels, but love makes up for all offenses (Proverbs 10:12).* Even when another adult leader is difficult to work with, use discretion; if necessary, follow the principles given to us in Matthew 18 to address any inappropriate conduct of another leader. Any other action will hurt the body of Christ.

CHAPTER 7

WHAT DO YOU DO WHEN THE UNEXPECTED HAPPENS

and trust me—you will face unexpected challenges!

When I think about events and retreats, I'm reminded of Moses. God referred to the Israelites as the "children of Israel," and Moses is a great biblical example of the many things that can go wrong on a youth event or retreat. If God had told Moses half of what would happen after leaving the "church parking lot" in Egypt, imagine how reluctant Moses would have been!

You will eventually face a moment during your retreat or event when things get a bit sticky. The bus (which has no A/C) breaks down on the way to summer camp. You lose the pastor's son at the amusement park. You planned a sports outreach for 50 teenagers—and 100 showed up. The unexpected *will* happen— so how can you prepare for something that's inevitable yet unknown until it actually happens? Ultimately, what matters is your attitude when things do go off course.

Here are some general ideas to guide you through these moments—especially the unexpected situations that might create problems for individuals or for your group.

Start here: Have some general emergency plans that leaders and students know. This should include a meeting place, because retreats and events often happen on unfamiliar turf.

Keep your eyes open: Groups of teenagers can be targeted when they are out of their normal elements. If a stranger enters your group while you're in a public space, contain and isolate them quickly. You can ask questions and determine the legitimacy of their proximity to the group after the immediate and unknown risk is removed.

Be a calming force: Panic will only escalate any tension already present in a crisis moment. Even when you are scared and don't have all the details, remain calm. Your levelheaded composure will help foster an environment where you and the other leaders can think clearly.

Be proactive: An OK plan executed at the right time may be better than a perfect plan executed too late! Be wise in your reactions, and find ways to address situations and handle problems before they escalate. If danger strikes on a trip with students, many people will judge your actions in hindsight, but don't let that paralyze you from taking action. Pray for God's lead through the Holy Spirit—after all, he has the big-picture perspective on any challenge you face!

Keep key documents: Bring along the students' permission slips and medical release forms, and know where they are. Don't leave them at home, and don't lose track of them while you're at your retreat or event.

It's a good idea that whoever has the medical release forms keep a cell phone on them—and it actually be turned on and they are reliable to answer it. Two years ago a student broke an arm at CIY and my secretary had our medical forms in her room. I called her because she was out on campus, and she quickly brought the student's form to me before the ambulance arrived. The first thing the medic said to me was, "Do you have a release for me to look at this young man?" I opened the binder, he looked the form over, and then he went to work on the student.

Communicate essentials: In an effort to decrease panic, communicate important and pertinent information. Use discretion; for instance, "Bad weather is coming, so we need to quickly take shelter" is better than "A tornado is coming here right now."

Here's a great system for keeping track of students in large groups. Hand each teenager an index card filled with important facts: their cell number, cabin/group leaders and their cell numbers, friends they bunk with, emergency contact information, and so on. When your group is stopping for gas or hitting the beach, no one is allowed off the bus or out of the van without giving the notecard to the leader—and once they climb back in, the leader redistributes the index cards. Leaders will know every person is there when all the notecards have been distributed. If notecards are left, then all the information needed to locate the students is right in your hand!

—Chad, Youth Leader

Wisely respond to bad news from home: Even though your group is away on a retreat or camp, life back at the ranch marches on. Tragic news may reach a student while you're there, particularly if you're away from home for a weekend or an entire week. When these moments happen, students need our attention. Take time to be with the teenager to pray and listen and comfort. Don't feel pressured to say the right thing. In most situations, there are no right words. The best gift you can give is your felt presence completely in the thick of the moment. Years later, the student may not remember the words you said or many other times you spent with them, but they will never forget the time you spent with them in their moment of difficulty.

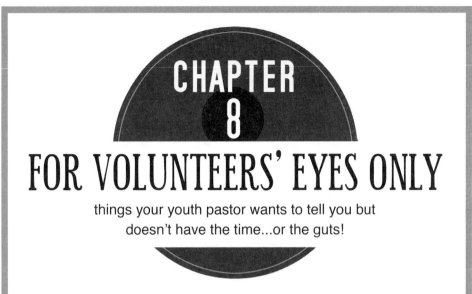

CHAPTER 8

FOR VOLUNTEERS' EYES ONLY

things your youth pastor wants to tell you but
doesn't have the time...or the guts!

- Please don't get our youth ministry or me in trouble.
  Drive safely.

- I have some of my own kids on this trip; I want and need
  you to be an adult!

- Don't complain about how little time I'm spending with you;
  it's about the students.

- I already feel unqualified compared to you because I don't
  have older kids myself, so please go easy.

- If you have frustrations with me or my decisions or my
  leadership style, please don't discuss those issues behind
  my back. Come to me first.

- When I'm talking to the students or giving vision for our
  ministry, please don't ridicule or undermine my leadership.

- Talk less about yourself, and spend more time listening to
  our teenagers.

- Be dependable. I'm reluctant to trust you with tasks because you have been inconsistent.

- You desire an upfront role in this ministry, but I can't put you there because you only attend special events—not regular services. You regularly talk negatively about our church leadership.

- The job you are doing is not more important than any other volunteer's job. In fact, the most important role any of us can fill at this retreat is hanging out with students. Make that your priority.

- Do the job you've been assigned or the role you requested. I cannot be the point person for every aspect of this event. The task is too large for one person to micro-manage every detail. When we all share the work, we all have more time to invest in our students.

CHAPTER 9

DON'T BE THIS PERSON

this isn't the way you want to earn a reputation in your ministry

Volunteers can slip into stereotypical roles during retreats and events because these roles are understandable and may seem easy or safe. Because well-meaning adults want to be known for something, they accept or untruthfully perpetuate an idea of who they are or how they want to be perceived. Like the students they lead, volunteers sometimes deal with issues of identity, too. This may stem from a need to be accepted or a fear of not having a place in the group. Whatever the underlying cause, these myopic roles are false images of the complex and wonderful people God has created.

Here are some unhealthy roles you might fall into that can harm your shepherding responsibility at events and retreats. Balance and moderation are key. We need some aspects of these roles—but only as seasoning, not the main course. Read through the list and see if you have fallen into one of these traps before. Commit the corresponding verse to memory as a tool to fight against these attitudes.

The Killjoy

Retreats and events should be fun. Teenagers can't help but get excited and a little rambunctious at the thought of a new adventure. Yes, they probably need to settle down, but watch your bark or you may damper the natural momentum of the group. *You will show me the way of life, granting me the joy of your presence and the pleasures of living with you forever (Psalm 16:11).*

The Enforcer

Consistent rules and structure are important to make any trip or event successful—but this must be balanced with love and mercy. An authoritarian view of leadership does not model correctly Jesus' role as our shepherd or the way volunteers should act toward the teenagers they lead. Have and enforce clear rules—but smile, too! *Always be humble and gentle. Be patient with each other, making allowance for each other's faults because of your love (Ephesians 4:2).*

The Herder

In most cases, teenagers participate in retreats and events because they choose to be there. They have lots of other options pulling for their time and attention. When they show up, it is usually because they still find value in being here. You want them to come back and get to know Jesus and his church, so don't treat them like cattle. *Care for the flock that God has entrusted to you. Watch over it willingly, not grudgingly—not for what you will get out of it, but because you are eager to serve God (1 Peter 5:2).*

Captain Condescending

Comments about how easy teenagers have it, how they dress, how poorly they eat, or other stereotypes can be real downers. Yes, students don't have the perspective at times to see the blessings they enjoy. But when they smell this underlying attitude, it is an automatic shutdown. *You must have the same attitude that Christ Jesus had. Though he was God, he did not think of equality with God as something to cling to. Instead, he gave up his divine privileges; he took the humble position of a slave and was born as a human being (Philippians 2:5-7).*

The Nicknamer

If you make it your personal agenda to give every person a nickname, the teenagers probably will return the favor by giving you a whole crop of really bad nicknames, too. A nickname is the kind of thing that should be developed over time by the whole group and not during one retreat or event by you. This is also only healthy when the recipient gives consent for the nickname, or else it can be viewed as a form of ridicule or disrespect.

The Prankster

As a youth worker, you have the opportunity to fight our culture's message of wild and crazy—especially for guys. The main reason you as a volunteer don't want teenagers pulling pranks is because things will get out of hand. This is inflated when an *adult* plays a prank on a student. It will divert people's attention and energy away from other, more meaningful moments. No matter how funny you think it is, the tradeoff is not worth it. Redirection is a great tool in this situation. Provide opportunities to do fun things that will mark students' experience while keeping them safe (and out of jail). *Too much activity gives you restless dreams; too many words make you a fool (Ecclesiastes 5:3).*

Dr. Negative

Drop the negative attitude. It won't help your teenagers, and it won't contribute to the team goal of creating a healthy, meaningful retreat or event. It also will alienate students and diminish any opportunity you may have to serve them. *"Let my teaching fall on you like rain; let my speech settle like dew. Let my words fall like rain on tender grass, like gentle showers on young plants" (Deuteronomy 32:2).*

The Matchmaker
This isn't the Love Boat; it's a youth event. Relationships are tough enough at this age, and most parents are trying to downplay the importance of romance in their teenagers' lives so they can concentrate on more important things for the time being—things like a deep, vibrant friendship with Jesus. So please don't live vicariously through the students. Yes, the topic will come up; yes, students will flirt. But the last thing you need is to make the focus of your event a dating game. *Teach me to do your will, for you are my God. May your gracious Spirit lead me forward on a firm footing (Psalm 143:10).*

Sir Extreme
Please don't be an extreme stunt leader who is always pushing the limits of rules and physical realities so teenagers will think you are cool. The rest of us leaders would prefer knowing about your plans to scale the outside of the building *before* you get to the third floor and need our help. God has called us on a great adventure, and there is a piece of God's adventurous spirit mirrored deeply in each of us. However, when you're dealing with teenagers who have varying levels of decision-making skills, don't portray a Mountain Dew® commercial lifestyle, or else the main focus on the event will get clouded. There is a time for adventure. Let's plan for it the best we can and not let it be the focus of all our time together. *"Physical training is good, but training for godliness is much better, promising benefits in this life and in the life to come" (1 Timothy 4:8).*

44

The Go-It-Aloner

Give other leaders the respect of good communication. Retreats and events can be difficult for leaders, and all of your decisions and actions affect the other members of your team. Consider how your leadership impacts the other leaders working with you. None of us can do it alone very effectively, and we always need more help. *Finally, all of you should be of one mind. Sympathize with each other. Love each other as brothers and sisters (1 Peter 3:8).*

Mr. or Ms. Vacation

We know you took vacation time to be at this retreat with all of us. Please don't make us all pay for that over and over again. *You must each decide in your heart how much to give. And don't give reluctantly or in response to pressure. "For God loves a person who gives cheerfully" (2 Corinthians 9:7).*

Captain Schedule

The schedule is intended to serve the people who are on the trip. When the schedule is no longer the best plan, re-evaluate and reschedule. If your key leader changes the plan, then go with the flow. Be flexible. Structure can be beneficial for teenagers, but it can also become stale and lifeless. Be careful not to serve the schedule over the students. *The Lord knows people's thoughts; he knows they are worthless! (Psalm 94:11).*

FIND YOUR ROLE

Now that we have covered some people you *shouldn't* be, here are some great roles your team needs! If you wait to be assigned a task, you may never get one. So ask for permission and be an initiator. Many volunteers find their ideal roles for serving because they recognize a need and meet it. Look for gaps; where can you make the difference? Don't underestimate your giftedness and what you bring to the whole group! At the same time, don't let your role define you. Yes, you will have tactical roles during events and retreats, but the long-range goal is to connect on a deeper level with a teenager.

The Prayer
Be the person who offers some wise, God-honoring advice in the middle of craziness: "Hey! Let's stop and pray about this!" Your group needs you if it's your natural inclination to be the one to stand up and lead in this area.

Dr. Hunch
Every leader needs a team member who picks up on vibes. An American Indian proverb says, "Listen to the whispers and you won't have to listen to the screams." Movements and trends start out in your group subtly. Some of us are oblivious to the finer tones and gestures in verbal and nonverbal communication. If you are gifted in sensing the temperament of individuals and the group, then help other leaders know when to love more, listen better, and step in.

Captain Communication
Retreats and events can move at the speed of light. Many leaders have good intentions of keeping parents back home informed, but they get busy. You can serve in an important role if you are gifted in this area. Create a website or special Facebook® page to provide timely updates. Having one person master the communication with folks back home can keep the real story straight!

God has created each person uniquely, and it takes all of our gifts to make a trip successful. A trip needs many roles for success: nurses, tech people, navigators, chefs, drivers, encouragers, and more! There are too many to list. Find the perfect role for your gifts, and then dive in!

CHAPTER 10

SPECIAL SITUATIONS THAT WILL COME UP

The dating couple

Be aware of the general rules concerning dating in your ministry. There are many different approaches. Here are some ideas that work well in most contexts: As the adult, de-escalate the situation by not joining in on the unfolding drama. Refocus the attention of the group toward something else. Don't make the couple feel like they are bad or not welcome because they are dating (don't take the angle that dating is bad).

The homesick student

It's likely that some of your teenagers will get homesick, especially if you're away for a week or longer. Many situations can quickly catapult well-balanced teenagers into extreme cases of emotional or physical sickness. By their very nature, events and retreats physically and emotionally drain teenagers—and adults, too. Be on guard for signs from students that point to abnormal behavior, eating habits, or sleeping patterns. Discretely intervene and talk with a homesick student, without drawing attention to the situation. Ask general questions about sleep schedule and diet, and find ways to encourage and uplift

47

the student. And along those lines—if you've established a rule banning cell phone use but you find that a homesick teenager has called Mom or Dad for a comforting conversation, it's probably a time to demonstrate some grace. Fighting a battle over the rule will likely be too big of a distraction.

Money
Teenagers are going to run out of money before the end of the event. This may be a law of nature, in fact.

The catfight
When teenagers get tired or bored, they're more likely to bicker. It happens—and it's not just a girl issue. Any student consumed by the daily gossip, fights, and clique news will live on a rollercoaster during an event or retreat. Decide now to remove yourself as a player in these escapades. You can't afford to engage in gossip, an unfair argument, or the reality of cliques. Choosing to engage in those activities will hinder your ability to speak truth into the lives of teenagers when they need it most. However, keep a close eye on situations that threaten to spin out of control and derail the entire group. You and other leaders may need to intervene to help resolve conflict.

The leadership card
There is no doubt that some teenagers are positioned and created to lead. But if you aren't careful, you may find yourself expecting much out of these students and watching them consistently to prove they are capable. Use caution when putting continued pressure on students with leadership ability. They will drop the ball. All teenagers make mistakes. They want to be one of the kids, too. Know when to pull back on the pressure.

The counseling moments

What do you do when students tell family secrets—including secrets like molestation at home? I don't have enough time here to go into all the details about a youth worker's legal responsibility in this area, but if any student shares details with you about abuse or violence, talk to your youth pastor or key leader; this person should be trained to know how to appropriately respond. Don't try to solve the problem yourself, and don't promise a teenager that you won't pass along their secrets. You are not a trained psychologist, and youth ministries can be damaged if they don't appropriately respond or pass along such allegations to authorities. While at retreats and events, encourage other healthy adult relationships, share information with others when appropriate or required, protect yourself, never counsel the opposite sex, don't keep secrets, hold conversations in open areas, and don't let the situation become the whole trip's experience.

I had a student make the accusation that her dad had choked her with his hands and pushed her down. I knew some details about the family (her parents are split) and her situation, and I knew that I am a mandated reporter. I called the mom and told her that her daughter was having a great week but she had been sharing some serious stuff on her heart. I asked her mom for the guardian ad-litem's phone number to talk about this. Her mom gave it to me, and I called her and asked for advice. In all situations we need to remember that we are a mandated reporter, but when we report something we are putting a family at great vulnerability and we better have good discernment about that student and their accusation and whether they are trustworthy. Some things need to wait until home and others need to be dealt with immediately. I know when I get home I check out because I have trip comp time, then wrapping up rentals from the trip, cleaning up youth ministry supplies, catching up on email, Facebook®, and so on. Then I remember three days later I had better do something about that accusation at camp.

—A Youth Leader

CHAPTER
II
THE LANDING

("Landing" is a term invented by early marketers to describe the experience of falling from the sky, like in a crash, when crazy things can happen—just saying)

We spend so much time planning our events and retreats, but sometimes the *landing* gets the least bit of attention. What happens after we have done all the hard work of actually making an event or retreat happen? Here are some thoughts.

Teenagers don't always want to land
Remember that some students are *not* excited about returning to their routines after an event or retreat—especially if they've built stronger relationships, developed new friendships, or experienced God's love in a meaningful way. They also may not be eager to get back home. Be sensitive to this. This is one reason it's good to get to know the stories of the teenagers you are ministering to. Their home life may not be something they are looking forward to stepping back into. Prepare teenagers for the reality they are about to face. Their friends and family members weren't there; they didn't witness the amazing

experience the teenagers had at this event or retreat. Getting re-acclimated into the reality of home may be easy—but it also may present challenges that can diminish students' excitement levels and commitments they may have made.

Connect with parents

Engaging parents is a key to helping your event's message leave a lasting impact. Put some thought into involving parents in a positive way after your event or retreat. Give them outlines of the topics you covered, questions that can fuel dialogue at home, and encouragement as they fulfill their vital role in spiritually leading their teenagers. Even parents who aren't followers of Christ still want to help their teenagers get the most out of their experiences. Assume that parents want to know what is going on and how they can maximize the investment in their child's life.

Whenever I get home from a big event or retreat, students are tired, I am tired, and everyone just wants to get their luggage and head home. And I want nothing more than for teenagers to get into the cars so I can leave and go home, too. So prolonging the drop-off time is something I try to avoid. Students are not ready for a prayer circle or another quick programming element. I am interested in having cookies if a parent or youth leader could take that responsibility on. I think of the landing at the event itself. When I get home, if I can get the students organized to do anything it's usually to help clean out the vehicles and help take things to the student center. Maybe the landing could be a parent page explaining the event to parents that you hand out with a warm cookie. Some ideas have been floating around about the youth pastor coming home early to a parent meeting to quickly explain the details of the trip to parents before they pick up their kids. This is a good landing. Maybe the landing is two-pronged: a student landing and a parent landing. The student landing is what

Maintain a long-term perspective

The best results from events and retreats aren't always evident right away. A bad ending can seem to undo a whole week's worth of incredible moments. The good news about this truth is that a *great* landing to an OK event can change the perception of the whole event! The difficulties the students thought would ruin the experience can actually end up laying the groundwork for lasting memories. It sounds funny, but the story of when the bus broke down gets way more play than the times when everything went smoothly!

Helping students take part of the event home with them is another important goal that will help you maintain a long-term perspective. Help your teenagers understand what it means to apply the things learned on the trip. It's more than feeling good about what they did, saw, or discussed as a group. It's about following God's lead and direction. It's about becoming the men and women God created them to be. Continue the momentum of the community you developed.

Remind everyone of the highlights

As a volunteer, you may not be the person coordinating this post-event or post-retreat detail, but I'd encourage you to make sure that it happens. Gather as a group after your event or retreat—a few days later, or a week later, or a month later. Enjoy a meal together and talk about what you learned and how your life is different. Retreats and events plant so many seeds in teenagers' lives, but there is never enough time to nurture every area of new growth. With all the energy and time put into making your event a success, there is usually a lot more to glean or mine.

Here are some other easy ideas that will keep those budding opportunities from falling through the cracks:

- Write letters to your students—during your event, on the ride home, or while the moment is fresh in your mind. Mail the letters a week after the trip.

- Send an email with the best pictures a few days after getting home, and ask your teenagers what stands out most in retrospect.

- Create a Facebook® page where students can share their memories and moments from your retreat.

Work with other volunteers and leaders to consider additional ways that you can extend the payoff of your event. The plan you come up with should reflect your own context. Forecast, communicate, and make provisions for the plan to become a reality.

We started asking students to take notes so they could give a testimony about their experience. Right now we have students scheduled to give a testimony about many experiences, sermons, or events we have had in the past. This is great because it turns into a testimony for other students to hear, it gives testimony-givers a chance to grow in their faith, and it turns into a trip announcement for the next year. This has been great for us, and our students have responded really well to the testimonies. Teenagers want to be challenged. Giving them the opportunity to listen and record thoughts with another purpose in mind can be huge.

Evaluate your success
Because you want and need to maintain a long-term perspective, you might not always know right away if an event or retreat is truly "successful." That word, of course, also depends on your team's definition of success. Was the event designed to introduce your youth ministry to unchurched teenagers in your community? Was the retreat intended to guide your students toward a deeper relationship with God or to find ways to live out their faith more tangibly?

As a volunteer, you're part of a team evaluating your event's success. If things didn't go as planned, have conversations about what could have been done differently. If the intended result didn't occur but you can point to other positive outcomes, draw other leaders' attention to that fact.

If an event didn't work well or didn't really fit into your youth ministry's philosophy, your team may need to ask the question, "Why are we doing this event?" You might need to cut it or change it completely. Often the best events are next-level exercises that lead teenagers to experience or apply lessons already being discussed in other areas of the ministry. When there is a consistent flow from the event to other areas in your ministry, the impact will always be greater. A small tweak may completely change the results.

So don't judge the success of an event too quickly. You may even want to put a moratorium on talking about it with church leaders and other volunteers until everyone on your team has had a shower and rest for perspective. Be careful not to jump to conclusions too quickly about what worked and what didn't.

CHAPTER 12
WRAPPING IT UP

A caution

You may not see results. You may not get thanked or recognized. You may get hurt by teenagers or other youth workers. If this happens to you, please get back up and know that you are in good company. *Yet he was merciful and forgave their sins and did not destroy them all. Many times he held back his anger and did not unleash his fury! (Psalm 78:38).*

A nudge

The window of opportunity to speak into teenagers' lives doesn't have to close. Once you have invested so much, you can still give a nudge. Satan will try to convince you that the weeklong camp experience with that teenager long ago doesn't register anymore. Don't underestimate what God can do through your obedience. A handwritten note with a word of encouragement can water or harvest a seed planted long ago. Listen to the Holy Spirit, the helper who lives inside you, and be open to walking the long road.

Protect your heart

Just like dogs and bees can smell fear, teenagers can smell fake people. If you sincerely love them, they will know and eventually respond. Making an impact takes dedication. Posturing your heart humbly before God will make all the difference in the world. Continually ask God to mold and shape your heart after your event or retreat. Don't be afraid to also ask God to gift you in new ways as you work with students.

Think ahead

Your investment will pay off for a long time to come. Being a volunteer can skyrocket relationships to the next level in one weekend, creating trust, shared experiences, and authentic relationships. Your involvement as a volunteer communicates that you are not too busy or too "good" to spend time with teenagers. You chose to submit yourself to enter into their world.

Because of the intensity of a retreat or event, a teenager who attends can cover more ground there, relationally speaking, than in weeks or months of Sunday school, small group, or midweek youth services. That one individual can build deep relationships with leaders and other teenagers. The payoff then continues every time the group meets because of the bridges that were built.

When you work with teenagers as a volunteer for events and retreats, know that you are not alone. This great calling is close to the heart of God, who puts his Spirit in us. The investment you make will yield incredible results. May God continue to grant you wisdom, patience, and the occasional glimpse of the harvest we are indeed reaping for his name!

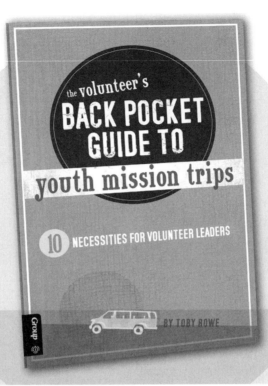

The Volunteer's Back Pocket Guide to Youth Mission Trips

10 Necessities for Volunteer Leaders

By Toby Rowe

Unlock the secrets to a successful mission experience with *The Volunteer's Back Pocket Guide to Youth Mission Trips.* This useful, practical book will guide you through the sometimes rough but always rewarding waters of a short-term mission trip. **You'll discover how to connect with your students, how to prepare for the unexpected, and how to savor those priceless moments you only find on a mission trip.**

Teenagers aren't the only people whose lives are changed on mission trips. The tips and wisdom found in this book will help you return home a different person—a person who has discovered the power of serving others and sharing the incredible message of Jesus.